ILLUMINATING THOUGHTS
ON THE ART OF LIVING

Timeless WISDOM

A Treasury of Universal Truths

COMPILED BY

GARY W. FENCHUK

with Leslie Davis

＊ ☾ ＊

CAKE EATERS INCORPORATED

COVER DESIGN: Lisa Burnett Bossi and Andrea Alban Gosline,
FineLine Marketing & Design
PRODUCTION: Carl Gosline, *Tiger Type Graphic Design & Printing*

COVER PHOTOGRAPH: © 1998 by Kallan Nishimoto

PUBLISHED BY: Cake Eaters, Inc. 14700 Village Square Place,
Midlothian, VA 23112. 1-888-9WISDOM

ISBN #: 0-9644902-3-4 paperback
        0-9644902-4-2 hardback (case bound)
        0-9644902-5-0 leather

Printed and bound in the United States of America

To Christy and Jason,

who have helped me understand
the real essence of life:
Love is central; people, not things,
are important;
and the moment is now.

A N D

To Mom,

"What the mother sings to the cradle
goes all the way down to the coffin."
Henry Ward Beecher (1813– 87)

With deepest love and respect,
thank you for being such a perfect role model.
(Sorry it didn't all stick...)

TABLE OF CONTENTS ———————

ACKNOWLEDGEMENTS ————————

Quotation books have become a dime a dozen as of late. Mostly, these publications are characterized by their quantity rather than their quality.

With this in mind, I wished to make certain that *Timeless Wisdom* did not become just another mediocre collection of personal favorites without universal appeal. To this end, I employed a unique concept of vigorous market-testing. This process was accomplished through a selective group of individuals that I dubbed the "Committee of 25." These participants expended countless hours, assessing and ranking the multitude of prospective quotations. Unquestionably, their insightful feedback tempered my own highly fallible judgement and helped distill these thoughts into the best quotation book ever published.

I am extremely indebted to these individuals and wish to acknowledge their crucial contribution. The committee was comprised of: Mike Beato, J.B. and Lois Campbell, Tom Carr, Bob and Linda Cary, Roland Diaz, Brenda Etheridge, Dorothy Fenchuk, Patti Fenchuk, Mark and Karen Fredrichs, Jo Frierson, Robbie Rice, Patti Hegdal, Eric and Judy Johnson, Brian and Pat Kracht, Liz Paul, Kathy Pearson, Roger Perry, Franny Powell, Louise Robinson, Bob Russell, Bette Schmidt, Roy and Barbara Sutton, Linda Tincher, Nan Walters, Catherine Weill, Leslie Davis Blackwell, Maryse Hotchkiss, Shannon Duke, Barbara Hennings, Clem Carlisle and Jim Beckner.

In particular, I would like to recognize and thank two individuals for their extraordinary commitment and dedication to this undertaking. Patti Hegdal, a long-time friend, and Mike Beato, my brother-in-law, contributed endless hours of wisdom and expertise and effectively served as co-editors on this publication.

Additionally, I find it imperative to cite the behind-the-scenes, but highly creative, tireless efforts of several individuals: Leslie Davis Blackwell, Grace Doucet, Connie Pollard, Debbie Gordon, Shirl Lowery, Liz Heuple, Nan Walters, Andrea Gosline, and Lisa Bossi, who helped convert an unorganized mountain of notecards into a highly professional and marketable product.

And last, but not least, I would like to acknowledge the ultimate contribution of my wife Patti, who has had to endure twenty-six years of living with a frustrated philosopher. Through it all, she amazingly has managed to remain loving, encouraging and supportive.

Colors fade, temples crumple, empires fall, but wise words remain.

Thorndike

Ever since my college days, I have been an avid student of philosophy and quotations. Like so many others, I have been searching for the meaning of life – and ultimately the secret to personal happiness and self-fulfillment. During my thirty-year quest, I have consulted hundreds of books and reviewed tens of thousands of quotations. While I have not yet uncovered any single 'magic bullet,' I have 'discovered' a multitude of enlightened eternal truths and universal values which have profoundly enriched my life.

My first major philosophical revelation came about as I read Dr. Maxwell Maltz's book, *Psycho-Cybernetics*. Maltz asserts that the mind is like a computer; once our brain becomes programmed with certain core beliefs, this 'input' dictates our thoughts, emotions, reactions, and actions (the output). This illuminating insight, that "you are what you think," propelled me to seek out and embrace the most positive, constructive, inspiring and empowering perspectives. My goal was to optimally reprogram my own personal 'computer.'

Ultimately, I have synthesized the nearly 700 thoughts found in *Timeless Wisdom* into a superior and powerful personal philosophy of life. These principles have helped me unravel some of life's most perplexing paradoxes, riddles and mysteries.

Indeed, in the process, I believe I have discovered the ever-elusive secret to true happiness. I first learned (all too slowly) that true, lasting happiness is not to be confused with momentary, superficial pleasure, nor is it a function of accumulating material possessions. Instead, I came to realize that the key to achieving everlasting happiness involves an enlightened four-prong approach: 1) understanding and loving others; 2) being virtuous and serving others; 3) living life fully and in the present; and 4) adopting an indomitable spirit of thankfulness. Quotations underscoring this perspective are found throughout the book.

Most quotation books seem designed to elicit a 'feel good' reaction – albeit of temporary and superficial dimensions. In contrast, *Timeless Wisdom* is a quotation book with an attitude. It is filled with simple, yet sometimes harsh, truths on how to live life optimally. You will find many of these thoughts to be penetrating, provocative, and even haunting. However, if one approaches the content with an open mind and invests the necessary time and effort, I believe *Timeless Wisdom* has the capacity to be a life-changing book.

"For a small reward a man will hurry away on a long journey, while for eternal happiness man will hardly take a single step."
Thomas à Kempis (1380 – 1471), adapted

I am totally convinced that if you imbue your mind with these immutable laws of life – embracing and incorporating these ideals into your daily life – you <u>will</u> live a rich, meaningful and happy life. It is as simple as that.

"The truth knocks on the door and you say, 'Go away, I'm looking for the truth' and so it goes away. Puzzling."

Robert M. Pirsig

I would like to add a couple of final notes regarding my motive for writing this book. In my thirty-year search for a definitive book which captures the wisdom of the ages, I was utterly frustrated by the non-existence of such a book. After I encountered this quote: "If you can't find the book you wish to read, write it," I became indefatigably resolved to compile *Timeless Wisdom*.

However, my most compelling reason for self-publishing *Timeless Wisdom* is simply a desire to share. The wisdom within the book has magically and permanently transformed my life. Quite literally, it has become my bible and has served as an infinite source of comfort, joy and guidance. As such, I feel a moral obligation to share the fruits of my philosophical journey.

"If wisdom were offered me with the proviso that I should keep it shut and refrain from declaring it, I should refuse. There's no delight in owning anything unshared."

Seneca (4 B.C.– A.D.65)

G.W.F.

The books that help you most, are those which make you think the most.

Theodore Parker (1810 – 60)

Man's mind, stretched to a new idea, never goes back to its original dimensions.

Oliver Wendell Holmes, Jr. (1841–1935)

Nothing in life is more exciting and rewarding than the sudden flash of insight that leaves you a changed person, not only changed, but for the better.

Arthur Gordon

Men stumble over the truth from time to time, but most pick themselves up and hurry off as if nothing happened.

Sir Winston Churchill (1874 –1965)

KEY

 the four directions (EARLY CHRISTIAN)

 viva!, live! (ITALIAN)

 fire (HITTITE)

 active intellect (UNKNOWN ORIGIN)

 potential energy (TIBETAN)

 sun sign; happiness (NATIVE AMERICAN)

 hindrance to overcome (EARLY ALCHEMY)

 independent movement (CELTIC)

 growth (ROMAN)

 goodwill (NEOLITHIC)

 grounding (EGYPTIAN)

 continuity (GAULISH)

xiii

CHAPTER 1

CHOOSING

ONE'S BELIEFS

Perhaps it would be a good idea, fantastic as it sounds, to muffle every telephone, stop every motor and halt all activity for an hour some day to give people a chance to ponder for a few minutes on what it is all about, why they are living and what they really want.

James Truslow Adams (1878 – 1949)

The life which is unexamined is not worth living.

Plato (427 – 347 B.C.)

Everything has been figured out except how to live.

Jean-Paul Sartre (1905 – 80)

All men should strive to learn before they die — what they are running from, and to, **and why**.

James Thurber (1894 – 1961)

We are all tattooed in our cradles with the beliefs of our tribe. You cannot educate a man wholly out of the superstitious fears which were implanted in his imagination, no matter how utterly his reason may reject them.

Oliver Wendell Holmes, Sr. (1809 – 94)

We live in a world of many illusions and much of human belief and behavior is ritualized nonsense.

Wes "Scoop" Nisker

To a large degree 'reality' is whatever the people who are around at the time agree to.

Milton H. Miller

A great many people think they are thinking when they are only rearranging their prejudices.

William James (1842 – 1910)

The truth will set you free. But before it does, it might make you angry.

Jerry Joiner, adapted

If you make people think they're thinking, they'll love you; but if you really make them think, they'll hate you.

Don Marquis (1878 – 1937)

He who will not reason is a bigot; he who cannot is a fool; and **he who dares not is a slave.**

Sir William Drummond (1585 – 1649)

We can easily forgive a child who is afraid of the dark; the real tragedy of life is when adults are afraid of the light.

Plato (427 – 347 B.C.)

I'm going to turn on the light, and we'll be two people in a room looking at each other and wondering why on earth we were afraid of the dark.

Gale Wilhelm

Come to the edge, He said. They said: we are afraid. Come to the edge, He said. They came. He pushed them, and they flew ...

Guillaume Apollinaire (1880 – 1918)

The high-minded man must care more for what's right than for what people think.

Aristotle (384 – 22 B.C.), adapted

The philosophies of one age have become the absurdities of the next, and the foolishness of yesterday has become the wisdom of tomorrow.

Sir William Osler (1849 – 1919)

Perhaps in time the so-called Dark Ages will be thought of as including our own.

G. C. Lichtenberg (1742 – 99)

A great-souled hero must transcend the slavish thinking of those around him.

Friedrich Nietzsche (1844 – 1900)

Perhaps it would be a good idea, fantastic as it sounds, to muffle every telephone, stop every motor and halt all activity for an hour some day to give people a chance to ponder for a few minutes on **what it is all about, why they are living and what they really want.**

James Truslow Adams (1878 – 1949)

Being extremely honest with oneself is a good exercise.

Sigmund Freud (1856 – 1939)

Why not spend some time in determining what is worthwhile for **us**, and then go after that?

William Ross

Every man must find his **own** philosophy . . . his attitude toward life.

Lin Yutang (1895 – 1976)

A man who does not think for himself does not think at all.

Oscar Wilde (1854 – 1900)

I don't want you to follow me or anyone else. I would not lead you into the promised land if I could, because if I could lead you in, somebody else would lead you out.

Eugene V. Debs (1855 – 1926)

No man is free who is not master of himself.

Epictetus (A.D. 60 – 110)

This above all; **to thine own self be true,** And it must follow, as the night the day, Thou canst not then be false to any man.

Shakespeare (1564 – 1616)

Poor is the man whose pleasures depend upon the permission of another.

Madonna

Be good enough to remember that your morals are only your habits; and do not call other people immoral because they have other habits.

George Bernard Shaw (1856 – 1950)

Infidel: In New York, one who does not believe in the Christian religion; in Constantinople, one who does.

Ambrose Bierce

Selfishness is not living as one wishes to live, it is asking others to live as one wishes to live.

Oscar Wilde (1854 – 1900)

Do not let your peace depend on the hearts of men; whatever they say about you, good or bad, you are not because of it another man — for as you are, you are.

Thomas à Kempis (1380 – 1471)

If your happiness depends on what somebody else says (or does), I guess you do have a problem.

Richard Bach

What you think of yourself is much more important than what others think of you.

Seneca (4 B.C. – A.D. 65)

I cannot give you the formula for success, but I can give you the formula for failure — try to please everybody.

Herbert Bayard Swope (1882 – 1958)

Is it so bad then to be misunderstood? Pythagoras was misunderstood, and Socrates, and Jesus, and Luther, and Copernicus, and Galileo, and Newton, and every pure and wise spirit that ever took flesh. To be great is to be misunderstood.

Ralph Waldo Emerson (1803 – 82)

Live 20% outside the 'proper' zone; remember that the great wise men of the past held no respect for today's conventions, and neither will the great men of the future.

Anonymous

The truly great consider first, how they may gain the approbation of God; and secondly, that of their own conscience; **having done this,** they would then willingly conciliate the good opinion of their fellowmen.

Charles Caleb Colton (1780 – 1832)

Do **well and right** and let the world sink.

Author Unknown

Do what you feel in your heart to be right for you will be criticized anyway. You will be damned if you do, and damned if you don't.

Eleanor Roosevelt (1884 – 1962)

Great tranquility of heart is his who cares for neither praise nor blame.

Thomas à Kempis (1380 – 1471)

Either control your own destiny, or someone else will!

John F. Welch, Jr.

You cannot always control your circumstances, but you can always control your own thoughts.

Charles E. Popplestone, adapted

The happiness of your life depends upon the quality of your thoughts.

Marcus Antonius (A.D. 86 – 161)

We create our fortune, for so the universe was wrought. **Thought is another name for fate;** choose then your destiny and wait, for **love brings love, and hate brings hate.**

Henry Van Dyke (1852 – 1933)

The soul becomes dyed with the color of its thoughts.

Marcus Aurelius (A.D. 121 – 180)

The game of life is the game of boomerangs. Our thoughts, deeds and words return to us sooner or later, with astounding accuracy.

Florence Shinn

Watch your thoughts; they become words.
Watch your words; they become actions.
Watch your actions; they become habits.
Watch your habits; they become character.
Watch your character; it becomes your destiny.

Frank Outlaw

Watch your **core beliefs**; they control your thoughts.

G.W.F.

13

A belief is not merely an idea that the mind possesses; it is an idea that possesses the mind.

Robert Bolton

The most powerful thing you can do to change the world is to **change your own beliefs** about the nature of life, people and reality to something more positive . . . **and begin to act accordingly.**

Shakti Gawain

People seem not to see that their opinion of the world is also a confession of character.

Ralph Waldo Emerson (1803 – 82)

As a man thinketh in his heart, so is he.

Proverbs 23:7

All that we are is the result of what we have thought. The mind is everything. **What we think, we become.**

Buddha (563 – 483 B.C.)

When you rule your mind you rule your world. When you choose your thoughts you choose results.

Imelda Shanklin

CHAPTER 2

LIVING LIFE
TO ITS FULLEST

My own experience has taught me this: if you wait for the perfect moment when all is safe and assured it may never arrive. Mountains will not be climbed, races won or lasting happiness achieved.

Maurice Chevalier (1888 – 1972)

Life is a paradise for those who love many things with a passion.

Leo Buscaglia

Follow your desire as long as you live; do not lessen the time of following desire, for the wasting of time is an abomination to the spirit.

Ptah-hotep (c. 2600 B.C.)
(oldest known author by name)

Time is infinitely more precious than money, and there is nothing common between them. You cannot accumulate time; you cannot borrow time; you can never tell how much time you have left in the Bank of Life. **Time is life . . .**

Israel Davidson (1870 – 1939)

Enjoy life — there are no re-runs.

Shirl Lowery

First I was dying to finish high school and start college.

And then I was dying to finish college and start working.

And then I was dying to marry and have children.

And then I was dying for my children to grow old enough so I could return to work.

And then I was dying to retire.

And now, I am dying . . . and suddenly realize **I forgot to live.**

Author Unknown

Life is not lost by dying; **life is lost minute by minute**, day by dragging day, in all the thousand small uncaring ways.

Stephen Vincent Benét (1898 – 1943)

Resolved: To live with all my might while I do live, and as I shall wish I had done ten thousand ages hence.

Jonathan Edwards (1703 – 58)

Start by admitting from cradle to tomb, it isn't that long a stay.

Liza Minnelli, Cabaret

My own experience has taught me this: if you wait for the perfect moment when all is safe and assured it may never arrive. Mountains will not be climbed, races won or lasting happiness achieved.

Maurice Chevalier (1888 – 1972)

He who hesitates is a damned fool.

Mae West (1892 – 1980)

The follies which a person regrets most in his life are those he didn't commit when he had the opportunity.

Helen Rowland (1876 – 1950)

Water which is too pure has no fish.

Ts'ai Ken T'an

If I had my life to live over again, I'd try to make more mistakes next time. I would relax. I'd be sillier than I have been on this trip. I would climb more mountains, swim more rivers and watch more sunsets. I would have more actual troubles and less imaginary ones. Oh, I've had my moments, and if I had to do it over again, I'd have more of them. In fact, **I'd try to have nothing else, just moments, one after another** . . . I would pick more daisies.

Nadine Stair (at age 89)

Live as you will have wished to have lived when you are dying.

Charles F. Gellert

There was a wise man in the Easata whose constant prayer was that he might see today with **the eyes of tomorrow**.

Alfred Mercier

Imagine returning to the misty past from the distant future. Embrace and savor life **now** as you would . . .

Anonymous

A person will be called to account on Judgment Day for every permissible thing he might have enjoyed but did not.

Talmud

The 11th commandment: Thou shalt be happy.

Author Unknown

If your morals make your life dreary, depend upon it: they are wrong.

Robert Louis Stevenson (1850 – 94), adapted

What is alive, and open, and active, is good. All that makes for inertia, lifelessness, dreariness, is bad. This is the essence of morality.

D. H. Lawrence (1885 – 1930)

Life is too important to be taken too seriously.

Oscar Wilde (1854 – 1900), adapted

Maybe you are here on earth to learn that life is what you make it, and it's to be enjoyed.

Dick Sutphen

The most wasted of all days is that during which one has not laughed.

Nicolas Chamfort (1741 – 94)

The art of being happy lies in the power of extracting happiness from common things.

Henry Ward Beecher (1813 – 87)

Life is a great and wondrous mystery, and the only thing we know that we have for sure is what is right here right now. **Don't miss it**.

Leo Buscaglia

Keep in mind this daily notion: **There are no ordinary moments**.

Dan Millman, adapted

If we could see the miracle of a single flower clearly, **our whole life would change**.

Buddha (563 – 483 B.C.)

Do you qualify to be alive or is the limit of your senses so as only to survive . . . ?

Ray Stevens, Mr. Businessman

God is always filling us with endless opportunities and sources of happiness . . . we just keep leaking.

Dan Millman, adapted

The moment one gives close attention to anything, even a blade of grass, it becomes a mysterious, awesome, indescribably magnificent world in itself.

Henry Miller (1891 – 1980)

The world is full of wonders and miracles but man takes his little hand and covers his eyes and sees nothing.

Israel Baal Shem

We take for granted the miraculous dance of creation, but the truly enlightened continuously see it **as if for the first time**.

Wes "Scoop" Nisker, adapted

If the stars should appear but one night every thousand years how man would marvel and adore.

Ralph Waldo Emerson (1803 – 82), adapted

The real voyage of discovery consists not in seeing new landscapes but in having new eyes.

Marcel Proust (1871 – 1922)

I have often thought it would be a blessing if each human being were stricken blind and deaf for a few days during his early adult life. Darkness would make him more appreciative of sight; silence would teach him the joys of sound.

Helen Keller (1880 – 1968)

To be blind is bad, but worse it is to have eyes and not to see.

Helen Keller (1880 – 1968)

Take time to marvel at the wonders of life.

G.W.F.

Don't hurry. Don't worry. You're only here on a short visit, so don't forget to stop and smell the roses.

Walter Hagan (1892 – 1969)

Is this the little girl I carried; is this the little boy at play? I don't remember growing older . . . when did they? When did she grow to be a beauty; when did he grow to be so tall? Wasn't it yesterday when they were small? Sunrise, sunset, sunrise, sunset . . . quickly flow the days.

Fiddler on the Roof

Teach your children to remind you, "But, . Daddy, I'm only going to be young once!"

Anonymous

I close my eyes, only for a moment . . . and the moment's gone.

Kansas, Dust in the Wind

You better take a fool's advice — take care of your own; 'cause one day they're here, next day they're gone.

Don Henley, New York Minute

Savor the smiles and laughter of your children — there is **nothing** more important.

G.W.F.

All the wonderful things in life are so simple that one is not aware of their wonder until they are beyond touch. Never have I felt the wonder and beauty and joy of life so keenly as now in my grief that Johnny is not here to enjoy them. Today, when I see parents impatient or tired or bored with their children, I wish I could say to them, "but they are alive, think of the wonder of that! They may be a care and a burden, but think, they are alive! You can touch them — **what a miracle!**"

Frances Gunther

There are only two ways to live your life. One is as though nothing is a miracle. The other is as though everything is a miracle.

Albert Einstein (1879 – 1955)

29

To be alive, to be able to see, to walk, to have houses, music, paintings — it's all a miracle. **I have adopted the technique of living life from miracle to miracle**.

Arthur Rubinstein (1887 – 1982)

Cherish your yesterdays; dream your tomorrows; but **live your todays!**

Author Unknown

There will come a day when you'd trade all of your tomorrows for a single yesterday. Enjoy these 'yesterdays' fully.

Anonymous

Oh, to be seventy again!

Oliver Wendell Holmes, Jr. (1841 – 1935)
(Said in his 87th year, while watching a pretty girl)

That man is a success who has lived well, laughed often and loved much.

Robert Louis Stevenson (1850 – 94)

CHAPTER 3

ROMANCING
THE PRESENT

I don't know what tomorrow will bring — except old age and death — but I do know that I do have today, one absolutely glorious day that I will savor and make the most of as if it were my last one . . . because it may be!

G.W.F. (1946 – 1998?)

Focus on today. Tomorrow is but a fantasy; yesterday is but a memory. **Today is the only reality.**

Anonymous

The secret of health for both mind and body is not to mourn for the past, nor to worry about the future, but to live the present moment wisely and earnestly.

Buddha (563 – 483 B.C.)

A magical perspective: If, in your mind, you can bring up the drawbridges on yesterday and tomorrow and **restrict yourself to today** . . . your cares will evaporate and your joys will skyrocket.

Anonymous

Stay present. You'll always have time to worry later on if you want to.

Dan Millman

Forever is but a trail of 'Nows'. The best a man can do is live every one fully in its turn.

Author Unknown

I don't know what tomorrow will bring — except old age and death — but I do know that I do have today, one absolutely glorious day that I will savor and make the most of as if it were my last one . . . because it may be!

G.W.F. (1946 – 1998?)

Death plucks my ears and says, "Live, I am coming."

Oliver Wendell Holmes, Jr. (1841 – 1935)
(Radio address on his ninetieth birthday)

Depend upon it, Sir, when a man knows he is to be hanged in a fortnight, it concentrates his mind wonderfully.

Samuel Johnson (1709 – 84)

I should like to enjoy this summer flower by flower, as if it were to be the last one for me.

André Gide (1869 – 1951)

You don't get to choose how you're going to die. Or when. You can only decide how you're going to live. **Now**.

Joan Baez

Enjoy yourself. These **are** the good old days you're going to miss in the years ahead.

Author Unknown

These are magic years . . . and therefore magic days . . . and therefore magic moments.

Anonymous

We don't remember days; we remember moments.

Cesare Pavese (1908 – 50)

Life is nothing but a series of moments. Start living the moments and the years will take care of themselves.

G.W.F.

Life can only take place in the present moment. If we lose the present moment, we lose life.

Buddha (563 – 483 B.C.)

It's only possible to live happily ever after on a **moment-to-moment** basis.

Margaret Bonnano

In **every moment**, the quality of your life is on the line. In each, you are either fully alive or relatively dead.

Dan Millman

Every moment is a golden one for him who has the vision to recognize it as such.

Henry Miller (1891 – 1980)

For you, the world is weird because if you're not bored with it you're at odds with it. For me the world is weird because it is stupendous, awesome, mysterious, unfathomable. I want to convince you that **you must learn to make every act count**, since you are going to be here for only a short while; in fact, too short for witnessing all the marvels of it.

Don Juan (Carlos Castaneda), adapted

Do not delay; the golden moments fly!

Henry Wadsworth Longfellow (1807 – 82)

Every now and then, I become absolutely obsessed with the moment . . . but not nearly enough.

Anonymous

There is only the moment. The now. Only what you are experiencing at this second is real. This does not mean you live **for** the moment. It means you live **in** the moment.

Leo Buscaglia

We all cling to the past or long for the future, making us unavailable to the present.

Bhagwan Shree Rajneesh, adapted

As you walk and eat and travel, **be where you are**. Otherwise you will miss most of your life.

Buddha (563 – 483 B.C.)

Great is the man who has not lost his child-like heart.

Mencius (371 – 288 B.C.)

On Arturo Toscanini's eightieth birthday, someone asked his son, Walter, what his father ranked as his most important achievement. The son replied, "For him there can be no such thing. Whatever he happens to be doing at the moment is the biggest thing in his life — whether it is conducting a symphony or peeling an orange."

Ardis Whitman

You're searching, Joe, for things that don't exist; I mean beginnings. Ends and beginnings — there are no such things. **There are only middles**.

Robert Frost (1874 – 1963)

The little things? The little moments? They aren't little.

Jon Kabat-Zinn

The only way to live is to accept each minute as an unrepeatable miracle, which is exactly what it is — a miracle and unrepeatable.

Margaret Storm Jameson

All the gold in the world cannot buy a dying man one more breath — so what does that make today worth?!

Og Mandino (1923 – 96), adapted

Every day is my best day; **this is my life.** I'm not going to have this moment again.

Bernie Siegel

Life lived for tomorrow will always be just a day away from being realized.

Leo Buscaglia

Gather ye rosebuds while ye may,
Old Time is still a-flying;
And this same flower that smiles today,
To-morrow will be dying.

Robert Herrick (1591 – 1674)

May you live all the days of your life.

Jonathan Swift (1667 – 1745)

CHAPTER 4

THE ART OF
POSITIVE THINKING

Your living is determined not so much by what life brings you as by the attitude you bring to life; not so much by what happens to you as by the way your mind looks at what happens.

Lewis L. Dunnington

The greatest discovery of my generation is that **a human being can alter his life by altering his attitude of mind.**

William James (1842 – 1910)

Act as if you were already happy and that will tend to make you happy.

Dale Carnegie (1888 – 1955)

Our self image and our habits tend to go to-gether. Change one and you will automatically change the other.

Dr. Maxwell Maltz (1899 – 1975)

There is a basic law that **like attracts like.** Negative thinking definitely attracts negative results. Conversely, if a person habitually thinks optimistically and hopefully, his positive think-ing sets in motion creative forces — and success instead of eluding him flows toward him.

Norman Vincent Peale (1898 – 1994), adapted

46

The world is what we think it is. **If we can change our thoughts, we can change the world.**

H. M. Tomlinson (1873 – 1958)

Let one therefore keep the mind pure, for what a man thinks, that he becomes.

The Upanishads (900 – 600 B.C.)

By your thoughts you are daily, even hourly, building your life; you are carving your destiny.

Ruth Barrick Golden

Life does not consist mainly, or even largely, of facts and happenings. It consists mainly of the storm of thoughts that are forever blowing through one's mind.

Mark Twain (1835 – 1910)

Your living is determined not so much by what life brings you as by the attitude you bring to life; not so much by what happens to you as by the way your mind looks at what happens.

Lewis L. Dunnington

If you permit your thoughts to dwell on evil, you yourself will become ugly.

Paramahansa Yogananda

And, if your friend does evil to you, say to him, "I forgive you for what you did to me, but how can I forgive you for what you did — to yourself?"

Friedrich Nietzsche (1844 – 1900)

We are our own devils; we drive ourselves out of our Edens.

Johann Wolfgang von Goethe (1749 – 1832)

We can choose to see life as a series of trials and tribulations, or we can choose to see life as an accumulation of treasures.

Author Unknown

Every life has its dark and cheerful hours. Happiness comes from choosing which to remember.

Author Unknown

The mind is like a river; upon its waters thoughts float through in a constant procession every conscious moment. You stand on a bridge over it and can stop and turn back any thought that comes along. **The art of contentment is to let no thought pass that is going to disturb you.**

Dr. Frank Crane (1861 – 1928), adapted

The art of being wise is the art of knowing what to overlook.

William James (1842 – 1910)

Remember, no one can make you feel inferior (or anything else) without your consent.

Eleanor Roosevelt (1884 – 1962), adapted

Nobody has the right to wreck your day, let alone your life. And guess what? Nobody does, you do . . .

G.W.F.

I have had more trouble with myself than with any man I have ever met.

Dwight Moody (1837 – 99)

To be wronged is nothing unless you continue to remember it.

Confucius (551 – 479 B.C.)

He who harbors a slight will miss the haven of happiness.

Author Unknown

It is not possible for the human mind to hold both a positive and negative thought at the same time.

Lily Tomlin, adapted

Every tomorrow has two handles. You can take hold of the handle of anxiety or the handle of enthusiasm. **Upon your choice so will be your day.**

Author Unknown

And so will be your **life**.

G.W.F.

One man has enthusiasm for 30 minutes, another for 30 days, but it is the man who has it for 30 years who makes a success of his life.

Edward B. Butler (1612 – 80)

A man can succeed at almost anything for which he has unlimited enthusiasm.

Charles Schwab

When a man dies, if he can pass enthusiasm along to his children, he has left them an estate of incalculable value.

Thomas Edison (1847 – 1931)

Given the three thousand million years of **chance occurrences** leading up to the chance encounter of one egg and one sperm that leads to the one cell that becomes you or me . . . **the mere fact of existing should keep us all frozen in a contented dazzlement of surprise.**

Opus, Outland

There is a Tibetan story about an old, blind turtle who lives in the depths of the ocean. Once every thousand years, the turtle swims to the top of the sea, and sticks its head up through the waves, surfacing for air. Now imagine that there is a wooden ring floating somewhere on the surface of the ocean, and think of how rare it would be for the blind turtle, coming up for air once every thousand years, to put its head through the wooden ring. **It is just that rare, say the Tibetans, for a being to gain human birth.**

Chop Wood, Carry Water

53

Celebrate your existence!

> *William Blake (1757 – 1827)*

Life for every person should be a journey in jubilance!

> *Charles Fillmore (1854 – 1948)*

Just think how happy you would be if you lost everything you have right now, and then got it back again.

> *Author Unknown*

It is not how much we have, but **how much we enjoy**, that makes happiness.

> *Charles H. Spurgeon (1834 – 92)*

He enjoys much who is thankful for little; a grateful mind is both a great and a happy mind.

> *Thomas Secker*

If the good Lord took me tomorrow, I have already been luckier than any man has a right to be. Anything else is pure gravy.

G.W.F.

There is no one luckier than he who thinks himself so.

German proverb

Gratitude is not only the greatest of virtues, but the mother of all the rest.

Cicero (106 – 43 B.C.)

There's a 'magic switch' inside all of us which can transform the worst to the best (or the best to the worst). It should be everyone's ultimate goal to discover and master this mechanism.

Anonymous

If you are distressed by anything external, the pain is not due to the thing itself, but to your estimate of it; and this **you have the power to revoke at any moment.**

Marcus Aurelius (A.D. 121 – 180)

Our best friends and our worst enemies are our thoughts.

Dr. Frank Crane (1861 – 1928)

The mind is its own place, and in itself can make a heaven of hell, or a hell of heaven.

John Milton (1608 – 74)

The kingdom of God is within you.

Jesus

A wise man will be the master of his mind. A fool will be its slave.

Publilius Syrus (1st century B.C.)

56

Nothing is good or bad but that our thinking
makes it so.

Shakespeare (1564 – 1616)

Two men look out through the same bars; one
sees the mud and one the stars.

Frederick Langbridge (1849 – 1923)

Be your own palace or the world's your jail.

Author Unknown

The greater part of our happiness or misery
depends on our dispositions, and not on our
circumstances. We carry the seeds of the one or
the other about with us in our minds wherever
we go.

Martha Washington (1731 – 1802)

We do not see things as **they** are. We see them
as **we** are.

Talmud

The world is a great mirror. It reflects back what you are.

Thomas Dreier

A loving person lives in a loving world. A hostile person lives in a hostile world. Everyone you meet is your mirror.

Ken Keyes, Jr.

I have found that if you love life, life will love you back.

Arthur Rubinstein (1887 – 1982)

The trick is in what one emphasizes. We either make ourselves miserable, or we make ourselves happy. The amount of work is the same.

Don Juan (Carlos Castaneda), adapted

The real secret of happiness is simply this; to be willing to live and let live, and to know very clearly in one's own mind that **the unpardonable sin is to be an unpleasant person**.

Galen Starr Ross

We have but one life — whether we spend it laughing or weeping.

Author Unknown

This is the best day the world has ever seen. Tomorrow will be better.

R. A. Campbell

What a wonderful life I've had! I only wish I'd realized it sooner.

Colette (1873 – 1954)

CHAPTER 5

REALIZING ONE'S POTENTIAL

It is very dangerous to go into eternity with possibilities which one has oneself prevented from becoming realities. A possibility is a hint from God. One must follow it.

Sören Kierkegaard (1813 – 55)

When you get to the Great Grandstand in the sky and look down on this Game of Life, you will come to realize: **there were no limits** . . . !

G.W.F.

If you accept a limiting belief, then it will become a truth for you.

Louise Hay

According to the theory of aerodynamics, **the bumble bee is unable to fly**. This is because the size, weight and shape of its body in relation to the total wing spread **make flying impossible.** But the bumble bee, being ignorant of these profound scientific truths, goes ahead and flies anyway and manages to make a little honey every day.

Author Unknown

They can because they think they can.

Virgil (70 – 19 B.C.)

If you can dream it, you can do it.

Walt Disney (1901 – 66)

There is a giant asleep within every man.
When the giant awakes, miracles happen.

Frederick Faust (1892 – 1944)

I am free to be what I want to be and to do
what I want to do.

Jonathan Livingston Seagull (Richard Bach)

Nothing in the world can take the place of
persistence. Talent will not; nothing is more
common than unsuccessful men with talent.
Genius will not; unrewarded genius is almost a
proverb. Education will not; the world is full of
educated failures. Persistence and determina-
tion alone are omnipotent.

Calvin Coolidge (1872 – 1933)

63

Success is a little like wrestling a gorilla. You don't quit when you're tired — you quit when the gorilla is tired.

Robert Strauss

Do what you can, with what you have, where you are.

Theodore Roosevelt (1858 – 1919)

I am only one, but I am one. I cannot do everything; but I will not let what I cannot do interfere with what I can do.

Edward Everette Hale (1822 – 1909)

You've got to dance like there's nobody watching. You've got to love like you'll never get hurt. You've got to come from the heart if you want it to work.

Susanna Clarke

All the wonders you seek are within yourself.

Sir Thomas Brown (1605 – 82)

Oz never did give nothin' to the Tin Man that he didn't already have.

America, <u>Tin Man</u>

Within you right now is the power to do things you never dreamed possible. This power becomes available to you just as soon as you can **change your beliefs**.

Dr. Maxwell Maltz (1899 – 1975)

Believe that you have it, and you have it.

Latin proverb

So oftentimes it happens that we live our lives in chains and we never even know we have the key.

Eagles, <u>Already Gone</u>

It is very dangerous to go into eternity with possibilities which one has oneself prevented from becoming realities. **A possibility is a hint from God.** One must follow it.

Sören Kierkegaard (1813 – 55)

God gives food to every bird, but does not throw it into the nest.

Montenegrin proverb

The aim, if reached or not, makes great the life; Try to be Shakespeare, leave the rest to fate.

Robert Browning (1812 – 89)

Most people go to their graves with their songs still unsung.

Oliver Wendell Holmes, adapted

Death is not the greatest loss in life. The greatest loss is what dies inside of us while we live.

Norman Cousins (1915 – 90)

Do not let time pass without accomplishing something. Otherwise you will regret it when your hair turns gray.

Yue Fei

One must have the adventurous daring to accept oneself as a bundle of possibilities and undertake the most interesting game in the world — making the most of one's best.

Harry Emerson Fosdick (1878 – 1969)

Life is like a ten-speed bike. Most of us have gears we never use.

Charles M. Schulz

Make the most of yourself, for that is all there is of you.

Ralph Waldo Emerson (1803 – 82)

Regret for the things we did can be tempered by time; it is regret for the things we did not do that is inconsolable.

Sidney J. Harris

For all sad words of tongue or pen, the saddest are these: "It might have been."

John Greenleaf Whittier (1807 – 92)

This is the only chance you will ever have on earth with this exciting adventure called life. So **why not plan it**, and try to live it as richly, as happily as possible?

Dale Carnegie (1888 – 1955)

If we did all the things we are capable of doing, we would literally astonish ourselves.

Thomas Edison (1847 – 1931)

The original sin is to limit the IS. **Don't.**

Richard Bach

What keeps you from believing that the universe is yours? Reach out, embrace it. I say, **"the sky's the limit!"** So get your bag, get your stuff, and head for the stars . . . I'll meet you out there.

Maura Beatty

CHAPTER 6

IN SEARCH
OF HAPPINESS

The fountain of contentment must spring up in the mind. He who has so little knowledge of human nature as to seek happiness by changing anything but his own disposition will waste his life in fruitless efforts and multiply the grief which he purposes to remove.

Samuel Johnson (1709 – 84)

If you observe a really happy man, you will find him building a boat, writing a symphony, educating his son, growing double dahlias or looking for dinosaur eggs in the Gobi Desert. He will not be searching for happiness as if it were a collar button that had rolled under the radiator, striving for it as a goal in itself. He will have become aware that he is happy in the course of **living life twenty-four crowded hours of each day.**

W. Beran Wolfe (1900 – 35)

Happiness, in this world, if it comes at all, comes indirectly as a dividend. Make it the object of pursuit, and it leads us on a wild-goose chase, and is never attained.

Nathaniel Hawthorne (1804 – 64), adapted

My opinion is that you never find happiness until you stop looking for it.

Chuang-tzu (369 – 286 B.C.)

If my heart can become pure and simple like that of a child, I think there can be no happiness greater than this.

Kitaro Nishida (1870 – 1945)

O for a life of sensations rather than of thoughts!

John Keats (1795 – 1821)

If you are unhappy, you are too high up in your mind.

Carl Jung (1875 – 1961), adapted

In those moments when we forget ourselves — not thinking, "Am I happy?", but completely oblivious to our little ego — we spend a brief but beautiful holiday in heaven.

Eknath Easwaran

Why aren't you happy? It's because 99% of everything you do, and say, and think, is for yourself.

Wei Wu Wei (Terence Gray) (1895 – 1986)

To forget the self is to be enlightened by all things.

Kigen Dōgen (1200 – 53)

It is the paradox of life that the way to miss pleasure is to seek it first. The very first condition of lasting happiness is that a life should be full of purpose, aiming at something outside self.

Hugh Black

Many persons have a wrong idea of what constitutes true happiness. It is not attained through self-gratification but through fidelity to a worthy purpose.

Helen Keller (1880 – 1968)

Real joy comes not from ease or riches or from praise of men, but from doing something worthwhile.

Sir Wilfred Grenfell (1865 – 1940)

If you are suffering from a lack of self-worth, perhaps you are not doing anything worthwhile.

Anonymous

To be happy is easy enough if we give ourselves, forgive others, and live with thanksgiving. No self-centered person, no ungrateful soul can ever be happy, much less make anyone else happy. **Life is giving, not getting.**

Joseph Fort Newton (1880 – 1950)

If one only wished to be happy, this could be easily accomplished; but we wish to be happier than other people, and this is always difficult, for we believe others to be happier than they are.

Montesquieu (1688 – 1755)

Comparison is the death of true self-contentment.

John Powell

There are two things to aim at in life: first, to get what you want and, after that, to enjoy it. Only the wisest of mankind achieve the second.

Logan Pearsall Smith (1865 – 1946)

Don't let the good things of life rob you of the best things.

Maltbie D. Babcock

Who seeks more than he has hinders himself from enjoying what he has.

Solomon Ibn Gabirol (1021 – 58)

Compare what you want with what you have, and you'll be unhappy; compare what you have with what you deserve and you'll be happy.

Evan Esar

It is a great obstacle to happiness to expect too much.

Bernard de Fontenelle (1657 – 1757)

Contentment is a pearl of great value, and whoever procures it at the expense of ten thousand desires makes a wise and a happy purchase.

Balguy, adapted

The secret of contentment is knowing how to enjoy what you have, and to be able to lose all desire for things beyond your reach.

Lin Yutang (1895 – 1976)

God grant me the serenity to accept the things I cannot change, courage to change the things I can, and **the wisdom to know the difference**.

Reinhold Niebuhr (1894 – 1962), The Serenity Prayer

Never try to teach a pig to sing. It wastes your time and it just annoys the pig.

Author Unknown

It is the chiefest point of happiness that a man is willing to be what he is.

Desiderius Erasmus (1466 – 1536)

Happiness does not consist in having what you want, but wanting what you have.

Confucius (551 – 479 B.C.)

Praise and blame, gain and loss, pleasure and sorrow come and go like the wind. To be happy, rest like a giant tree in the midst of them all.

Buddha's Little Instruction Book

How things look on the outside of us depends on how things are on the inside of us. Remember, there is nothing wrong with nature; the trouble is in ourselves.

Parks Cousins

No matter what you are doing, keep the undercurrent of happiness. Learn to be secretly happy within your heart in spite of all circumstances.

Paramahansa Yogananda

When some **external** event raises your spirits, and you think good days are preparing for you, do not believe it. It can never be so. **Nothing can bring you peace but yourself**.

Ralph Waldo Emerson (1803 – 82)

There is nothing outside you. That is what you must ultimately learn.

A Course in Miracles

In the depth of winter, I finally learned that there was within me an invincible summer.

Albert Camus (1913 – 60)

I have noticed that folks are generally about as happy as they make up their minds to be.

Abraham Lincoln (1809 – 65)

Few things are needed to make the wise man happy, but nothing satisfies the fool; this is the reason so many of mankind are miserable.

Francois La Rochefoucauld (1613 – 80)

Happiness is a present attitude — not a future condition.

Hugh Prather

Remember happiness doesn't depend upon who you are or what you have; **it depends solely upon what you think.**

Dale Carnegie (1888 – 1955)

Like it or not, life is lived in and through the mind.

Anonymous

He who has so little knowledge of human nature as to seek happiness **by changing anything but his own disposition** will waste his life in fruitless efforts and multiply the grief which he purposes to remove.

Samuel Johnson (1709 – 84)

Joy is not in things; it is in us.

Richard Wagner (1813 – 83)

There is no value in life except what you choose to place upon it and **no happiness in any place except what you bring to it yourself**.

Henry David Thoreau (1817 – 62)

If you cannot be happy **here** and **now**, you never will be.

Taisen Deshimaru, adapted

Wherever I go, there I am.

Aristotle (384 – 22 B.C.)

Paradise is where I am.

Voltaire (1694 – 1778)

When we cannot find contentment in ourselves, it is useless to seek it elsewhere.

Francois La Rochefoucauld (1613 – 80)

I am never bored anywhere; being bored is an insult to oneself.

Jules Renard (1864 – 1910)

Happiness is not a state to arrive at, but a manner of traveling.

Samuel Johnson (1709 – 84)

The secret of life is **balance**, and the absence of balance is life's destruction.

Hazrat Inayat Khau

Nothing in excess.

Inscription in the Temple of Apollo
Delphi, Greece

Happiness is a way station between too little and too much.

Channing Pollock (1880 – 1946)

Happiness is found in the golden middle of two extremes.

Aristotle (384 – 22 B.C.)

The way to happiness: keep your heart free from hate, your mind from worry, live simply, expect little, give much.

Barney O'Lavin

True happiness flows from the possession of **wisdom and virtue** and not from the possession of external goods.

Aristotle (384 – 22 B.C.)

There is no happiness where there is no wisdom.

Sophocles (496 – 06 B.C.)

Happiness is the only good.

The time to be happy is now.

The place to be happy is here.

The way to be happy is to make others so.

Robert G. Ingersoll (1833 – 99)

CHAPTER 7

DEALING WITH ADVERSITY

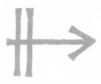

So I close in saying that I might have had a bad break, but I have an awful lot to live for. Today, I consider myself the luckiest man on the face of the earth.

Lou Gehrig (1903 – 41)

The mark of your ignorance is the depth of your belief in injustice and tragedy. What the caterpillar calls the end of the world, the Master calls the butterfly.

Richard Bach

God allows us to experience the low points of life in order to teach us lessons we could not learn in any other way.

C. S. Lewis (1888 – 1965)

Rules for Being Human:

- You will learn lessons.
- There are no mistakes — only lessons.
- A lesson is repeated until it is learned.
- If you don't learn easy lessons, they get **harder**. (Pain is one way the universe gets your attention.)
- You'll know you've learned a lesson when your actions change.

Author Unknown

Good people are good because they've come to wisdom through failure. We get very little wisdom from success, you know.

William Saroyan (1908 – 81)

We turn to God for help when our foundations are shaking, only to learn that it is God who is shaking them.

Charles C. West

We ask God for strength and God gives us difficulties to make us strong. We ask God for wisdom and God gives us problems.

Author Unknown

There is nothing the body suffers that the soul may not profit by.

George Meredith (1828 – 1909)

What doesn't kill me, makes me stronger.

Albert Camus (1913 – 60)

Many men owe the grandeur of their lives to their tremendous difficulties.

Charles H. Spurgeon (1834 – 92)

For everything you have missed, you have gained something else.

Ralph Waldo Emerson (1803 – 82)

When bad things happen, that's good. (When good things happen, you shouldn't need a philosophy.)

Mike Mathers, adapted

It has done me good to be somewhat parched by the heat and drenched by the rain of life.

Henry Wadsworth Longfellow (1807 – 82)

He that wrestles with us strengthens our nerves, and sharpens our skill. Our antagonist is our helper.

Edmund Burke (1729 – 97)

You have no friends; you have no enemies; you have only teachers.

Ancient saying

Everyone and everything around you is your teacher.

Ken Keyes, Jr.

I thank God for my handicaps, for, through them, I have found myself, my work, and my God.

Helen Keller (1880 – 1968)

Looking back, we see with great clarity, and what once appeared as difficulties now reveal themselves as blessings.

Dan Millman

Old age, to the unlearned, is winter; to the learned, it is harvest time.

Yiddish saying

I'm looking forward to looking back on all this.

Sandra Knell

We could never learn to be brave and patient if there were only joy in the world.

Helen Keller (1880 – 1968)

One often learns more from ten days of agony than from ten years of contentment.

Merle Shain

If you do not learn from your mistakes, you might just as well not make them.

Napolean Hill (1883 – 1970)

The gem cannot be polished without friction, nor man perfected without trials.

Chinese proverb

Failure is the greatest opportunity I have to know who I really am.

John Killinger

Make the most of every failure. Fall forward.

Author Unknown

Hard-won victories are the sweetest of all.

Lara McClellan

Who has never tasted what is bitter does not know what is sweet.

German proverb

Life is like a rollercoaster; the highs are meaningless but for the lows.

Anonymous

The word 'happiness' would lose its meaning if it were not balanced by sadness.

Carl Jung (1875 – 1961)

To be without some of the things you want is an indispensable part of happiness.

Bertrand Russell (1872 – 1970)

There is a legend of a comfort-loving man who died and was borne to the other world where every wish was gratified. No effort, no struggle was required of him. He became bored and said "I can't stand this everlasting bliss any longer; I want to feel there are things I cannot have. I want to go to hell." The attendant replied: "And where do you think you are, sir?"

Harry O. Ritter

To appreciate heaven well, 'tis good for a man to have some fifteen minutes of hell.

Will Carleton (1845 – 1912)

I cried because I had no shoes until I met a man who had no feet.

Persian saying

It is not what you have lost, but what you have left that counts.

Harold Russell

If you can't be thankful for what you receive, be thankful for what you escape.

Author Unknown

Take a mental walk through the cancer wards, the insane asylums, the homeless ghettoes, the children's hospitals . . . and then re-ask yourself what is bothering you.

G.W.F.

But for the grace of God, I could be a blind, crippled beggar in the streets of Calcutta.

Anonymous

If all our misfortunes were laid in one common heap whence everyone must take an equal portion, most people would be contented to take their own and depart.

Socrates (470 – 399 B.C.)

How dare you waste your life in self-pity. **Billions** of people gratefully would trade places with you!

Anonymous

Reflect upon your present blessings, of which every man has many; not on your past misfortunes, of which all men have some.

Charles Dickens (1812 – 70)

Happiness is not the absence of problems, but the ability to cope with them.

Author Unknown

If you can alter things, alter them. If you cannot, put up with them.

English proverb

Life is not the way it's supposed to be. It's the way it is. The way you cope with it is what makes the difference.

Virginia Satir

So I close in saying that I might have had a bad break, but I have an awful lot to live for. Today, I consider myself the luckiest man on the face of the earth.

Lou Gehrig (1903 – 41)

Life is mostly froth and bubble,
Two things stand like stone;
Kindness in another's trouble,
Courage in your own.

Adam Lindsay Gordon (1833 – 70)

Pain is inevitable. Suffering is optional.

M. Kathleen Casey

Suffering is simply the difference between what is and what I want it to be.

Dr. Spencer Johnson, adapted

All unhappiness is the result of excessive expectations.

Buddhist saying

For peace of mind, **resign as general manager of the universe**.

Larry Eisenberg

The sun will set without thine assistance.

Talmud

Beware of anxiety. Next to sin, there is nothing that so troubles the mind, strains the heart, distresses the soul and confuses the judgment.

William Ullathorne (1806 – 89)

Anxiety is a thin stream of fear trickling through the mind. If encouraged, it cuts a channel into which all other thoughts are drained.

Arthur Somers Roche

Worry often gives a small thing a big shadow.

Swedish proverb

Worry does not empty tomorrow of its sorrow; it empties today of its joy.

Author Unknown

One hour of worry is one hour of hell.

James Dodd

Worms eat you when you are dead; worries eat you when you're alive.

Jewish proverb

Drag your thoughts away from your troubles — by the ear, by the heels, or any other way you can manage it. It's the healthiest thing a body can do.

Mark Twain (1835 – 1910)

Save worry and anxiety for the major upsets in life. Today make a conscious effort to see something positive in every situation.

Author Unknown

Happy is the man who has broken the chains which hurt the mind, and **has given up worrying once and for all**.

Ovid (43 B.C. – A.D. 17)

You'll break the worry habit the day you decide you can meet and master the worst that can happen to you.

Arnold Glasgow

Remember — nothing will happen that you and God can't handle together.

Author Unknown

The worst sorrows in life are not in its losses and misfortune, but its fears.

A. C. Benson

It isn't the experience of today that drives men mad. It is the remorse for something that happened yesterday, and the dread of what tomorrow may disclose.

Robert Jones Burdette

When I look back on all these worries I remember the story of the old man who said on his deathbed that he had had a lot of trouble in his life, **most of which never happened**.

Sir Winston Churchill (1874 – 1965)

Golf without bunkers and hazards would be tame and monotonous. **So would life**.

B. C. Forbes (1880 – 1954)

We find no real satisfaction or happiness in life without obstacles to conquer and goals to achieve.

Dr. Maxwell Maltz (1899 – 1975)

One day, who knows? Even these hardships will be grand things to look back on.

Virgil (70 – 19 B.C.)

Rule #1 — Don't sweat the small stuff.
Rule #2 — It's almost all small stuff.

Robert S. Eliot, adapted

I saw somebody peeing in Jermyn Street the other day. I thought, is this the end of civilization as we know it? Or is it simply somebody peeing in Jermyn Street?

Alan Bennett

It's just a bad **day**, it's not a bad **life**. Smile!

Patti Hegdal

No one will ever get out of this world alive. Resolve therefore to maintain a reasonable perspective and sense of values.

Lloyd Shearer

Today the greens are greener, the clouds are puffier, **the things that are important are more important**, and the things that aren't have gone way down.

A man who escaped death

When your expectations for life are reduced to zero, then everything becomes more meaningful.

Dr. Stephen Hawking (reflecting on his terminal disease)

I realize now how precious each day is.

Coach Jim Valvano (as he was dying of cancer)

Once you have experienced the seriousness of your loss you will be able to experience the wonder of being alive.

Robert Veninga

That it will never come again is what makes life so sweet.

Emily Dickinson (1830 – 86)

Life . . . I absolutely love it and can't get enough of it!

G.W.F. (observed after the death of a loved one)

The confrontation with death . . . makes everything look so precious, so sacred, so beautiful that I feel more strongly than ever the impulse to live it, to embrace it, and to let myself be overwhelmed by it.

Abraham Maslow (1908 – 70)

A rainbow and a cuckoo's song may never come together again. May never come this side of the tomb.

W. H. Davies

Do not stand by my grave and weep.
I am not there. I do not sleep —
I am a thousand winds that blow,
I am the diamond glints on snow,
I am the sunlight on ripened grain,
I am the gentle autumn rain.
Do not stand by my grave and cry.
I am not there. I did not die.

Author Unknown (In memory of Dad, G.W.F.)

To live in hearts we leave behind is not to die.

Thomas Campbell (1777 – 1844)

What we have done for ourselves alone, dies with us. What we have done for others and the world, remains and is immortal.

Robert Pine

We ask for long life, but 'tis deep life, or grand moments, that signify.

> *Ralph Waldo Emerson (1803 – 82)*

Life is long if it is full.

> *Seneca (4 B.C. – A.D. 65)*

No man is in true health who can not stand in the free air of heaven, with his feet on God's free turf, and thank his Creator for the simple luxury of physical existence.

> *T. W. Higginson (1823 – 1911)*

The biggest lesson I've learned . . . was that if you have all the fresh water you want to drink and all the food you want to eat, **you ought never to complain about anything**.

> *Eddie Rickenbacker (1890 – 1973) after being adrift in the Pacific Ocean for 21 days*

108

The mere absence of any major problems at the present should be a cause, in and of itself, for euphoria.

Anonymous

Know that joy is rarer, more difficult, and more beautiful than sadness. Once you make this all-important discovery, you must embrace joy as a moral obligation.

André Gide (1869 – 1951)

There are 'problems' and there are **real problems**. The vast majority of us don't have **real problems**. Our failure to appreciate the difference constitutes a colossal distortion of thinking — which has served to effectively destroy more lives than all war and disease combined.

G.W.F.

To hate and to fear is to be psychologically ill. It is, in fact, the consuming illness of our time.

H. A. Overstreet

The greatest griefs are those we cause ourselves.

Sophocles (496 – 06 B.C.)

Ten enemies cannot hurt a man as much as he hurts himself.

Yiddish saying

Man, like a bridge, was designed to carry the **load of the moment**, not the combined weight of a year all at once.

William A. Ward

The human mind often seems addicted to 'awfulizing'. As soon as any particular problem does get resolved we become obsessed with replacing it with another — real or imaginary.

Anonymous

The few real evils of the moment can be either cured or endured; it is only countless imaginary evils in the future that make people anxiety-ridden for a lifetime.

Earl Nightingale, adapted

Our fears are more numerous than our dangers, and we suffer much more in apprehension than in reality.

Seneca (4 B.C. – A.D. 65)

He who fears he will suffer, already suffers from his fear.

Michel de Montaigne (1533 – 92)

111

To him who is in fear everything rustles.

Sophocles (496 – 06 B.C.)

If we let things terrify us, life will not be worth living.

Seneca (4 B.C. – A.D. 65)

Be of good cheer. Do not be afraid.

Jesus

Never bend your head. Always hold it high. Look the world straight in the eye.

Helen Keller (1880 – 1968)

However mean your life is, meet it and live it; do not shun it and call it hard names. It is not so bad as you are. The fault-finder will find fault even in paradise. **Love your life**.

Henry David Thoreau (1817 – 62)

I know what's happening in this world — there are liars and cheats, there's prejudice, violence, greed, sickness — I know what's happening. I'm not going to let it deter me from living my life, though. Look, I live in this world, and dammit, I'm going to be cheerful and positive about living in this world.

Joseph Raymond

With all its sham, drudgery and broken dreams, **it is still a beautiful world**. Be cheerful. Strive to be happy.

Desiderata (1692)

CHAPTER 8

TAKING RISKS

Twenty years from now you will be more
disappointed by the things you didn't do than
by the ones you did do. So throw off the bowlines. Sail away from the safe harbor. Catch the
trade winds in your sails. Explore. Dream.
Discover.

Author Unknown

115

Life is either a daring adventure — or it is nothing.

Helen Keller (1880 – 1968)

So often life is every bit as good, if not better, than the wonderful make-believe movies we love to watch. It has all the same joy and sorrow, mystery and suspense, adventure and excitement, and love and emotion — except it's real. Live your life as if it were a great movie — complete with the happy ending.

Anonymous

Life's a play; all the world's a stage; and you're the star!

Shakespeare (1564 – 1616), adapted

You know, we can't get out of life alive! We can either die in the bleachers or die on the field. We might as well come down on the field and **go for it**!

Les Brown

We are always getting ready to live, but never living.

Ralph Waldo Emerson (1803 – 82)

One of the most tragic things I know about human nature is that all of us tend to put off living.

Dale Carnegie (1888 – 1955)

I have spent my days stringing and unstringing my instrument, while the song I came to sing remains unsung to this day.

Rabindranath Tagore (1861 – 1941)

Why wait? Life is not a dress rehearsal. Quit practicing what you're going to do, and just do it. In one bold stroke you can transform today.

Marilyn Grey

Do the thing you fear and the death of fear is certain.

Ralph Waldo Emerson (1803 – 82)

Life shrinks or expands according to one's courage.

Anaïs Nin (1903 – 77)

Don't bunt. Aim out of the ballpark. Aim for the company of the immortals.

David Ogilvy

Don't let the fear of striking out hold you back.

Babe Ruth (1895 – 1948)
(Ruth held the all-time record for home runs
. . . and strikeouts!)

No man ever became great except through many and great mistakes.

William Ewart Gladstone (1809 – 98)

Defeat should never be a source of discouragement, but rather a fresh stimulus.

South

Failure is success if we learn from it.

Malcolm Forbes (1919 – 90)

Only those who dare to fail greatly can ever achieve greatly.

Robert F. Kennedy (1925 – 68)

How will you ever know if you can paint that picture, run that business, sell that vacuum cleaner, earn that degree, hold that office, make that speech, win that game, marry that girl, write that book, bake that souffle, build that house — unless you try it!

Richard M. DeVos

Since you have to do the things you have to do, be wise enough to do some of the things you want to do.

Malcolm Forbes (1919 – 90)

Go out on the limb — that's where the fruit is.

Will Rogers (1879 – 1935)

Mistakes are part of the dues one pays for a full life.

Sophia Loren

To try is to risk failure. But risk must be taken, as the greatest hazard in life is to risk nothing. **The person who risks nothing, does nothing, has nothing, and is nothing**.

Author Unknown

And the trouble is, if you don't risk anything, you risk even more.

Erica Jong

Failures are a normal part of life. They are not disasters.

Author Unknown

If your life is free of failures, you're not taking enough risks.

Author Unknown

Statistically — 100% of the shots you don't take, don't go in.

Wayne Gretzsky

Those who try to do something and fail are infinitely better than those who try to do nothing and succeed.

Richard Bird

Do not be too timid and squeamish about your actions. All life is an experiment.

Ralph Waldo Emerson (1803 – 82)

Every year that I live I am more convinced that the waste of life lies in the love we have not given, the powers we have not used, the selfish prudence which will risk nothing, and which, shirking pain, misses happiness as well.

Mary Cholomondeley

I know you're still afraid to rush into anything
. . . there're just so many summers, Babe, just
so many springs . . .

Don Henley, Last Worthless Evening

If one advances confidently in the direction of
his dreams, and endeavors to live the life which
he has imagined, he will meet with a success
unexpected in common hours.

Henry David Thoreau (1817 – 62)

First say to yourself what you would be; and
then do what you have to do.

Epictetus (A.D. 60 – 110)

What would you attempt to do if you knew
you could not fail?

Dr. Robert Schuller

123

Fear: the thief of dreams.

Author Unknown

Remember when you were at your best? Now be there again!

Author Unknown

Formulate and stamp indelibly on your mind a mental picture of yourself as succeeding. Hold this picture tenaciously. Never permit it to fade . . . your mind will seek to develop the picture.

Norman Vincent Peale (1898 – 1994)

Proceed as if success were inevitable.

Author Unknown

Success often comes from not knowing your limitations.

Frank Tyger

Make no little plans: they have no magic to stir men's blood . . . make big plans, aim high in hope and work.

Daniel H. Burnham (1846 – 1912)

Make your plans as fantastic as you like, because 25 years from now they will seem mediocre. You will wonder why you did not make them 50 times as great.

Henry Curtis

Twenty years from now you will be more disappointed by the things you didn't do than by the ones you did do. So throw off the bowlines. Sail away from the safe harbor. Catch the trade winds in your sails. **Explore. Dream. Discover.**

Author Unknown

I love to sail forbidden seas, and land on barbarous coasts.

Herman Melville (1819 – 91)

Man cannot discover new oceans until he has courage to lose sight of the shore.

Author Unknown

Opportunities do not come with their values stamped upon them. Every one must be challenged. A day dawns, quite like other days; in it a single hour comes quite like other hours; but in that day and in that hour **the chance of a lifetime faces us**.

Maltbie D. Babcock

There are periods when to dare is the highest wisdom.

William Ellery Channing (1780 – 1842)

Whatever you can do, or dream you can, **begin it**. Boldness has genius, power and magic in it.

Johann Wolfgang von Goethe (1740 – 1832)

The woods are lovely, dark and deep. But I have promises to keep. And miles to go before I sleep.

Robert Frost (1874 – 1963)

Rest not! Life is sweeping by; go and dare before you die.

Johann Wolfgang von Goethe (1740 – 1832)

In a world where death is the hunter, my friend, **there is no time for regrets or doubts.**

Don Juan (Carlos Castaneda)

CHAPTER 9

UNDERSTANDING
OURSELVES AND OTHERS

Resolve to be tender with the young, compassionate with the aged, sympathetic with the striving, and tolerant with the weak and the wrong. Sometime in life you will have been all of these.

Lloyd Shearer

When dealing with people, remember you are not dealing with creatures of logic, but with creatures of emotion, creatures bristling with prejudice and motivated by pride and vanity.

Dale Carnegie (1888 – 1955)

Since we tend to see ourselves primarily in the light of our **intentions**, which are invisible to others, while we see others mainly in the light of their **actions**, which are all that's visible to us, we have a situation in which misunderstanding and injustice are the order of the day.

J. G. Bennett (1795 – 1872), adapted

Were we fully to understand the reasons for other people's behavior, it would all make sense.

Sigmund Freud (1856 – 1939), adapted

How to gain, how to keep, how to recover happiness, is in fact for most people at all times **the secret motive for all they do and all they are willing to endure.**

William James (1842 – 1910)

Fred Sanford: Didn't you learn anything being my son? Who do you think I'm doing this all for?

Lamont Sanford: Yourself.

Fred: Yeah, you learned something.

Sanford and Son

From his cradle to his grave a man never does a single thing which has any first and foremost object but one — to secure peace of mind, spiritual comfort, for himself.

Mark Twain (1835 – 1910)

No man consciously chooses evil because it is evil; he only mistakes it for the happiness that he seeks.

Mary Wollstonecraft Shelley (1797 – 1851),
adapted

I am malicious because I am miserable; if any being felt emotions of benevolence toward me, I should return them a hundred fold.

Frankenstein Monster,
(Mary Wollstonecraft Shelley)

What do you call love, hate, charity, revenge, humanity, magnanimity, forgiveness? Different results of the one Master Impulse: The necessity of securing one's self-approval.

Mark Twain (1835 – 1910)

The deepest principle of human nature is the craving to be appreciated.

William James (1842 – 1910)

Men are not against you; they are merely for themselves.

Gene Fowler

Half of the harm that is done in this world is due to people who want to feel important . . . **they do not mean to do harm** . . . they are absorbed in an endless struggle to think well of themselves.

T. S. Eliot (1888 – 1965)

Be kind, for everyone you meet is fighting a hard battle.

Plato (427 – 347 B.C.)

If we could read the secret history of our enemies, we would find in each man's life a sorrow and a suffering enough to disarm all hostility.

Henry Wadsworth Longfellow (1807 – 82)

Understanding will bring you compassion.

Louise Hay

The more a man knows, the more he forgives.

Confucius (551 – 479 B.C.)

Rest assured that, generally speaking, others are acting in exactly the same manner that you would under exactly the same circumstances. Hence, be kind, understanding, empathetic, compassionate and loving.

G.W.F.

To view each individual as being as good and worthy as oneself — therein lies the ultimate challenge. And the ultimate joy.

Anonymous

Then I saw you through myself, and found we were identical.

Fakhr ad-din Iraqi (1211 – 89)

We all live with the objective of being happy; our lives are all different . . . and yet the same.

Anne Frank (1929 – 45)

When you try to understand everything, you will not understand anything. **The best way is to understand yourself, and then you will understand everything**.

Shunryu Suzuki (1870 – 1966)

To know others you do not have to go and knock on four billion separate doors. **Once you have seen your real Self, you have seen the Self in all.**

Eknath Easwaran

I observe myself and I come to know others.

Lao-tzu (604 – 531 B.C.)

I am the entire human race compacted together. I have found that there is no ingredient of the race which I do not possess in either a small way or a large way.

Mark Twain (1835 – 1910)

Treat people as if they were what they ought to be and you help them to become what they are capable of being.

Johann Wolfgang von Goethe (1749 – 1832)

Really great men have a curious feeling that the greatness is not in them, but through them. And they see something divine in every other man.

John Ruskin (1819 – 1900)

Rare is the person who can weigh the faults of others without putting his thumb on the scales.

Byron J. Langenfeld

When you see a good man, think of emulating him; when you see a bad man, **examine your heart**.

Chinese proverb

Men's hatreds generally spring from fear or envy.

Niccolò Machiavelli (1469 – 1527)

Until you have formed the habit of looking for the good instead of the bad there is in others, **you will be neither successful nor happy**.

Author Unknown

Once upon a time a man whose ax was missing suspected his neighbor's son. The boy walked like a thief, looked like a thief, and spoke like a thief. But the man found his ax while digging in the valley, and the next time he saw his neighbor's son, the boy walked, looked and spoke like any other child.

Lao-tzu (604 – 531 B.C.)

Today, find a way to make changes in yourself instead of someone else. Sometimes the results are the same.

Author Unknown

I find good people good. And I find bad people good — if I am good enough.

Lao-tzu (604 – 531 B.C.)

The only devils in the world are those running in our own hearts. That is where the battle should be fought.

Mahatma Gandhi (1869 – 1948)

We have met the enemy and he is us.

Pogo (Walt Kelly)

Love and pity and wish well to every soul in the world; hate nothing but the evil that stirs in your own heart.

William Law

Resolve to be tender with the young, compassionate with the aged, sympathetic with the striving, and tolerant with the weak and the wrong. **Sometime in life you will have been all of these**.

Lloyd Shearer

If you judge people, you have no time to love them.

Mother Teresa (1910 – 97)

God himself, sir, does not propose to judge a man until the end of his days.

Samuel Johnson (1709 – 84)

Judge not, that ye not be judged.

Jesus

When you judge someone, you don't define them, you define yourself.

Dr. Wayne Dyer

140

I tell you one thing — if you want peace of mind, **do not find fault with others**.

Sri Sarada Devi (1836 – 86)

You who want peace can find it only by complete forgiveness.

A Course in Miracles

If your life is not all you want it to be, it may be that you have some forgiving to do!

Author Unknown

One of the secrets of a long and fruitful life is to **forgive everybody everything** every night before you go to bed.

Bernard Baruch (1870 – 1965)

The only people to get even with are those who have helped you.

Author Unknown

One word frees us all of the weight and pain of life. That word is Love.

Sophocles (496 – 06 B.C.)

If you do not learn how to love, **everywhere you go, you are going to suffer**.

Eknath Easwaran

So when the shoe fits, the foot is forgotten;
when the belt fits, the belly is forgotten;
when the heart is right, 'for' and 'against' are forgotten.

Thomas Merton (1915 – 68)

Out beyond the ideas of right-doing and wrong-doing is a field — I'll meet you there.

Jelaluddin Rumi (1207 – 73)

We can judge others or we can love others —
but we can't do both.

Anonymous

I think the greatest thing in the world is to
believe in people.

John Galsworthy (1867 – 1933)

Experience has convinced me that there is a
thousand times more goodness, wisdom and
love in the world than men imagine.

Gehles

I hold to my ideals because, in spite of everything, I still believe that people are really good
at heart.

Anne Frank (1929 – 45)

CHAPTER 10

LOVING AND
SERVING OTHERS

I don't know what your destiny will be, but one thing I know: the only ones among you who will be truly happy are those who will have sought and found how to serve.

Albert Schweitzer (1875 – 1965)

145

Hatred does not cease through hatred at any time. **Hatred ceases through love**. This is an unalterable law.

Buddha (563 – 483 B.C.)

"What makes the lamb love Mary so?" the eager children cried. "Why Mary loves the lamb, you know," the teacher then replied.

Author Unknown

Love and you shall be loved. All love is mathematically just, as much as the two sides of an algebraic equation.

Ralph Waldo Emerson (1803 – 82)

Love is never lost. If not reciprocated, it will flow back and soften and purify the heart.

Washington Irving (1783 – 1859)

To forgive is the highest, most beautiful form of love. In return, you will receive untold peace and happiness.

Robert Muller

Forgiving means to pardon the unpardonable and loving means to love the unlovable. Or it is no virtue at all.

G. K. Chesterton (1874 – 1936)

A person's ability to forgive is in proportion to the greatness of his soul.

Author Unknown

The weak can never forgive. Forgiveness is the attribute of the strong.

Mahatma Gandhi (1869 – 1948)

He who has not forgiven an enemy has never yet tasted one of the most sublime enjoyments of life.

Johann K. Lavater (1741 – 1801)

The quality of mercy . . . is twice blessed. It blesseth him that gives and him that takes.

Shakespeare (1564 – 1616)

If you want others to be happy, practice compassion. If **you** want to be happy, practice compassion.

Dalai Lama

He who cannot forgive others destroys the bridge over which he himself must pass.

George Herbert (1593 – 1633)

When a deep injury is done to us, we never recover until we forgive.

Alan Paton

The person who pursues revenge should dig two graves.

Author Unknown

To hate another is to hate yourself.

Brian Adams

Self-love is not only necessary and good, it is a prerequisite for loving others.

Rollo May

What if I should discover that the poorest of the beggars and the most impudent of offenders are all within me, and that I stand in need of the alms of my own kindness; that I myself am the enemy who must be loved — what then?

Carl Jung (1875 – 1961)

If you cannot love yourself you cannot love others.

Neale Donald Walsch,
Conversations with God

Those who are at war with others are not at peace with themselves.

William Hazlitt (1778 – 1830)

Never, ever, engage in envy or hatred — it is a mental cancer that will only destroy oneself.

Anonymous

Anger is often more harmful than the injury that caused it.

Author Unknown

Those who hate you don't win unless you hate them back; and then you destroy yourself.

Richard M. Nixon (1919 – 94)

He who angers you, conquers you.

Elizabeth Kenny (1886 – 1952)

I shall allow no man to belittle my soul by making me hate him.

Booker T. Washington (1856 – 1915)

Beginning today, treat everyone you meet as if they were going to be dead by midnight. Extend to them all the care, kindness and understanding you can muster, and do with no thought of any reward. **Your life will never be the same again.**

Og Mandino (1923 – 96)

We should live in such a way that in our last hours we will not regret having loved too little.

Chiara Lubich

I wasn't there that morning when my father passed away . . . I didn't get to tell him all the things I had to say. I just wish I could have told him in the living years.

Mike & The Mechanics,
The Living Years

Why is it that only upon death, and at the funeral, we fully rejoice in the glory of each person's life and capture the true spirit of love . . . ? Let every day be doomsday!

G.W.F.

The way to love anything is to realize that it might be lost.

G. K. Chesterton (1874 – 1936)

If one were given five minutes warning before sudden death, five minutes to say what it had all meant to us, every telephone booth would be occupied by people trying to call up other people to stammer that they loved them.

Christopher Morley (1890 – 1957)

Call now.

G.W.F.

Life is short. Be swift to love! Make haste to be kind!

Henri F. Amiel (1821 – 81)

It is one of the most beautiful compensations of life that no man can sincerely try to help another without helping himself.

Ralph Waldo Emerson (1803 – 82)

Down in their hearts, wise men know this truth: the only way to help yourself is to help others.

Elbert Hubbard (1856 – 1915)

It is uncomfortable doctrine which the true ethics whisper into my ear: you are happy, they say; therefore you are called upon to give much.

Albert Schweitzer (1875 – 1965)

We have no more right to consume happiness without producing it than to consume wealth without producing it.

George Bernard Shaw (1856 – 1950)

You have not lived a perfect day, unless you have done something for someone who will never be able to repay you.

Ruth Smeltzer

The test of thankfulness is not what you have to be thankful for, but whether anyone else has reason to be thankful that you are here.

Author Unknown

Make it a rule . . . never, if possible, to lie down at night without being able to say, "I have made one human being at least a little wiser, a little happier or a little better this day."

Charles Kingsley (1819 – 75)

You will find, as you look back upon your life, that the moments that stand out are the moments when you have done things for others.

Henry Drummond (1851 – 97)

In about the same degree as you are helpful, you will be happy.

Karl Reiland

We make a living by what we get, we make a life by what we give.

Sir Winston Churchill (1874 – 1965)

He who receives a benefit should never forget it; he who bestows should never remember it.

Pierre Charron (1541 – 1603)

This is the final test of a gentleman: his respect for those who can be of no possible service to him.

William Lyon Phelps (1865 – 1943)

Real love begins where nothing is expected in return.

Antoine de Saint-Exupéry (1900 – 44)

Think of other people. Serve other people sincerely. No cheating . . .

Dalai Lama

If we bestow a gift or favor and expect a return for it, it is not a gift but a trade.

Author Unknown

Act with kindness, but do not expect gratitude.

Confucius (551 – 479 B.C.)

Donate anonymously — that is the ultimate and true spirit of charity.

Anonymous

Three things in human life are important: The first is to be kind. The second is to be kind. The third is to be kind.

Henry James (1843 – 1916)

No act of kindness, no matter how small, is ever wasted.

Aesop (c.550 B.C.)

If you want happiness for an hour – take a nap.

If you want happiness for a day – go fishing.

If you want happiness for a month – get married.

If you want happiness for a year – inherit a fortune.

If you want happiness for a lifetime – **help others**.

Chinese proverb

This giving – I hope it gets to be contagious because it feels so good . . . I've never been happier than I am today.

Ted Turner
(after donating $1 billion to worldwide charities)

CHAPTER 11

DEVELOPING VALUES

I once got a huge check. And the same day I got a huge hug and kiss from my child. The hug and kiss felt better.

G.W.F.

161

To love God truly, one must first love man. And if anyone tells you that he loves God and does not love his fellow man, you will know that he's lying.

Hassidic saying

When you hear a man say, "I hate," adding the name of some race, nation, religion, or social class, you are dealing with a belated mind. That man may dress like a modern, ride in an automobile, listen over the radio, but his mind is properly dated about 1000 B.C.

Harry Emerson Fosdick (1878 – 1969)

Hatred toward any human being cannot exist in the same heart as love to God.

Dean William Inge (1860 – 1954)

He does not believe who does not live according to his belief.

Thomas Fuller (1608 – 61)

Who you **are** shouts so loud, I cannot hear what you're saying.

Ralph Waldo Emerson (1803 – 82)

To say these words is nothing. But to mean these words is everything.

A Course in Miracles

Live truth instead of professing it.

Elbert Hubbard (1856 – 1915)

Men are all alike in their promises. It is only in their deeds that they differ.

Molière (1622 – 73)

Our problem is not to find better values but to be faithful to those we profess.

John W. Gardner

If one is to do good one must do it in the min-ute particulars. General good is the plea of the hypocrite, the flatterer and the scoundrel.

William Blake (1757 – 1827)

He who waits to do a great deal of good at once will never do anything. Life is made up of little things. True greatness consists in being great in little things.

Samuel Johnson (1709 – 84)

If, after I depart this vale, you ever remember me and have thought to please my ghost, for-give some sinner and wink your eye at some homely girl.

H. L. Mencken (1880 – 1956)

164

The smallest good deed is better than the grandest good intention.

Duguet

If you can't feed a hundred people, then feed just one.

Mother Teresa (1910 – 97)

The road to Hell is paved with good intentions; the road to Heaven is paved with good deeds.

Anonymous

When God measures a man, He puts the tape around the heart instead of the head.

Author Unknown

I shall tell you a great secret, my friend. Do not wait for the last judgment; it takes place every day.

Albert Camus (1913 – 60)

When it's all over, will you be able to look Him in the eye?

G.W.F.

In a community in which there is involuntary starvation every well-fed person is a thief.

Holbrook Jackson

Surplus wealth is a sacred trust which its possessor is bound to administer in his lifetime for the good of the community.

Andrew Carnegie (1835 – 1919)

If a rich man is proud of his wealth, he should not be praised until it is known how he employs it.

Socrates (470 – 399 B.C.)

A man's true wealth is the good he does in this world.

Muhammad (570 – 632)

To die rich is to have lived in vain.

J. Krishnamurti (1895 – 1986)

Sell whatever thou hath, and give it to the poor, and thou shalt have treasure in heaven; and come, take up the cross, and follow me.

Two sources: a carpenter from Nazareth and a street-corner 'crazy' in New York City

People in general are equally horrified at hearing the Christian religion doubted, and at seeing it practiced.

Samuel Butler (1835 – 1902)

Christianity might be a good thing if anyone ever tried it.

George Bernard Shaw (1856 – 1950)

True religion is the life we **live**, not the creed we profess.

J. F. Wright

If you are what you do, then when you don't you aren't.

Dr. Wayne Dyer

We have committed the Golden Rule to memory. Let us now commit it to life.

Edwin Markham (1852 – 1940)

What is bad to you, do not to others. That is the entire law; all the rest is commentary.

Rabbi Hillel (30 B.C. – A.D. 10)

I got a simple rule about everybody. If you don't treat me right — shame on you!

Louis Armstrong

No man is a true believer unless he desireth for his brother that which he desireth for himself.

Muhammad (570 – 632)

169

The world is my country; mankind is my brethren; **to do good is my religion**.

Thomas Paine (1737 – 1809)

Each man has a choice in life: he may approach it as a creator or a critic, a lover or a hater, a giver or a taker.

Author Unknown

The 'rules' of the Game of Life are for the winners to give some of it back to the losers . . .

Anonymous

You should never take more than you give in the Circle of Life.

Elton John, <u>Circle of Life</u>

"What goes around, comes around," . . . Make sure you are going to like what comes around!

Anonymous

Always do right. This will gratify some people, and astonish the rest.

Mark Twain (1835 – 1910)

There is never a wrong time to do the right thing.

Author Unknown

To see what is right and not do it is want of courage.

Confucius (551 – 479 B.C.)

In my humble opinion, non-cooperation with evil is as much a duty as is cooperation with good.

Mahatma Gandhi (1869 – 1948)

He who allows oppression shares the crime.

Erasmus Darwin (1731 – 1802)

If there is no justice, there is no peace.

Bahya ben Asher

It is the feeling of injustice that is insupportable to all men . . . No man can bear it or ought to bear it.

Thomas Carlyle (1795 – 1881)

You cannot trample upon people who are innocent and not expect retaliation.

Sylvester Stallone

172

White man turns the corner, finds himself within a different world; ghetto kid grabs his shoulder, throws him up against the wall. He says, "Would you respect me if I didn't have this gun, 'cause without it I don't get it and that's why I carry one."

Phil Collins, Both Sides of the Story

You can only protect your liberties in this world by protecting the other man's freedom. You can only be free if I am free.

Clarence Darrow (1857 – 1938)

Whoever claims a right for himself must respect the like right in another.

James Bryce (1838 – 1922)

How many years must a people exist before they're allowed to be free? How many times can a man turn his head and pretend that he just doesn't see?

Bob Dylan, Blowin' in the Wind

Neutral men are the devil's allies.

Edwin Hubbel Chapin

It is not only what we do, but also what we do not do, for which we are accountable.

Molière (1622 – 73)

The only thing necessary for the triumph of evil is for good men to do nothing.

Edmund Burke (1729 – 97)

Live so that when your children think of fairness, caring and integrity, they think of you.

H. Jackson Browne, Jr.

If you compare yourself with others you may become vain and bitter; for there will always be greater and lesser persons than yourself.

Desiderata (1692)

Humility is the most difficult of all virtues to achieve; nothing dies harder than the desire to think well of self.

T. S. Eliot (1888 – 1965)

If Christ was able to remain humble, perhaps the rest of us could also manage to do so.

Anonymous

How great some men would be if they were not arrogant.

Talmud

Nearly all men can stand adversity, but if you want to test a man's character, give him power.

Abraham Lincoln (1809 – 65)

A person is no longer great once he thinks he is so.

G.W.F.

Greatness flees from him who seeks it, and follows him who flees from it.

Talmud

Great minds discuss ideas, average minds discuss events, small minds discuss people.

Laurence J. Peter

The words of the tongue should have three gatekeepers:

- Is it true?
- Is it kind?
- Is it necessary?

Arabian proverb

Never say anything about others that you wouldn't want them to hear — because they probably will.

Anonymous

What you say tells other people what you are.

Author Unknown

Remember, what you possess in the world will be found at the day of your death to belong to someone else, but **what you are will be yours forever**.

Henry Van Dyke (1852 – 1933)

177

If you want to know how rich you really are, find out what would be left of you tomorrow if you should lose every dollar you own tonight.

William J. H. Boetcker

A man must seek his happiness and inward peace from objects which cannot be taken away from him.

Alexander Humboldt (1769 – 1859)

When wealth is lost, nothing is lost;
When health is lost, something is lost;
When character is lost, all is lost!

German proverb

Do not care overly much for wealth or power or fame, or one day you will meet someone who cares for none of these things, and **you will realize how poor you have become**.

Rudyard Kipling (1865 – 1936)

Do you know what real poverty is? It is never having a big thought or a generous impulse.

Jerome P. Fleishman

You will become as small as your controlling desire; as great as your dominant aspiration.

James Allen (1849 – 1925)

The **love** of money is the root of all evil.

St. Paul

It is the preoccupation with possession, more than anything else, that prevents man from living freely and nobly.

Bertrand Russell (1872 – 1970)

A man there was and they called him mad; the more he gave the more he had.

John Bunyan (1628 – 88)

Give, and it will be given to you.

Jesus

They who give have all things; they who withhold have nothing.

Hindu proverb

He who wishes to secure the good of others has already secured his own.

Confucius (551 – 479 B.C.)

The sage does not accumulate for himself. The more he gives to others, the more he possesses of his own. The way of Heaven is to benefit others and not to injure.

Lao-tzu (604 – 531 B.C.)

Superfluous wealth can buy superfluities only. Money is not required to buy one necessity of the soul.

Henry David Thoreau (1817 – 62)

Would you sell both your eyes for a million dollars . . . or your two legs . . . or your hands . . . or your hearing? Add up what you have, and you'll find that you wouldn't sell it all for all the gold in the world.

Dale Carnegie (1888 – 1955)

Measure wealth not by the things you have,
but by the things you have for which you
would not take money.

Author Unknown

What shall it profit a man, if he shall gain the
whole world, and lose his own soul?

Jesus

The Chinese tell of a man of Peiping who
dreamed of gold, much gold, his heart's desire.
He rose one day and when the sun was high
he dressed in his finest garments and went to
the crowded market place. He stepped di-
rectly to the booth of a gold dealer, snatched a
bag full of gold coins, and walked calmly away.
The officials who arrested him were puzzled:
"Why did you rob the gold dealer in broad
daylight?" they asked. "And in the presence of
so many people?" "**I did not see any
people**," the man replied. "**I saw only gold.**"

Louis Binstock

I don't think God put you on this earth just to make millions of dollars and ignore everything else.

Chris Amundsen

How men toil to lay up riches which they never enjoy.

William Jay

If we did but know how little some enjoy of the great things that they possess, there would not be much envy in the world.

Young

Even though you have ten thousand fields, you can eat no more than one measure of rice a day. Even though your dwelling contains a hundred rooms, you can use but eight feet of space a night.

Chinese proverb

Those who want much, are always much in
need.

Horace (65 – 8 B.C.)

True contentment depends not upon what we
have; a tub was large enough for Diogenes, but
a world was too little for Alexander.

Charles Caleb Colton (1780 – 1832)

He who is not contented with what he has
would not be contented with what he would
like to have.

Socrates (470 – 399 B.C.)

To know when you have enough is to be rich.

Lao-tzu (604 – 531 B.C.)

I once got a huge check. And the same day I got a huge hug and kiss from my child. The hug and kiss felt better.

G.W.F.

Keep the gold and keep the silver, but give us wisdom.

Arabian proverb

CHAPTER 12

CLOSING THOUGHTS

"**Y**our task . . . to build a better world," God said. I answered, "How? . . . this world is such a large, vast place, and there's nothing I can do." But God in all His wisdom said, "just build a better you."

Author Unknown

Just one great idea can completely revolution-ize your life.

Earl Nightingale (1921 – 89)

Any powerful idea is absolutely fascinating — and absolutely useless unless we choose to use it.

Richard Bach

All truly wise thoughts have been thought already thousands of times; but to make them truly ours, we must think them over again honestly, till they take root in our personal experience.

Johann Wolfgang von Goethe (1740 – 1832)

Good thoughts are no better than good dreams if you don't follow through.

Ralph Waldo Emerson (1803 – 82)

What we think, or what we know, or what we believe, is in the end, of little consequence. The only thing of consequence is what we **do**.

John Ruskin (1819 – 1900)

After all, it's what we do that makes us what we are.

Jim Croce, One Less Set of Footsteps

What good is it if a man claims to have faith but has no deeds?

James 2:14

Words are nothing but words; power lies in deeds. Be a person of action.

Mali Oriot Mamadu Konyate

If we do not change our daily lives, we cannot change the world.

Thich Nhat Hanh

Be ashamed to die until you have won some victory for mankind.

Horace Mann (1796 – 1859)

I will act as if I do make a difference.

William James (1842 – 1910)

Let everyone sweep in front of his door and the whole world will be clean.

Mother Teresa (1910 – 97)

"Your task . . . to build a better world," God said. I answered, "How? . . . this world is such a large, vast place, and there's nothing I can do." But God in all His wisdom said, **"just build a better you."**

Author Unknown

Live every day as if it were your last. **Treat everybody else as if he were you.**

Author Unknown

Be such a man, and live such a life, that if every man were such as you, and every life a life like yours, this earth would be God's Paradise.

Phillips Brooks (1835 – 93)

Love your enemies, bless them that curse you, do good to them that hate you.

Jesus

However many holy words you read, however many you speak, what good will they do if you do not act upon them?

The Dhammapada

Wisdom is knowing what to do next; **virtue is doing it**.

David Starr Jordan (1851 – 1931)

No longer talk at all about the kind of man a good man ought to be, but be such.

Marcus Aurelius (A.D. 121 – 180)

To laugh often and much, to win the respect of intelligent people and the affection of children; to earn the appreciation of honest critics and endure the betrayal of false friends; to appreciate beauty; to find the best in others; to leave the world a bit better, whether by a healthy child, a garden patch or a redeemed social condition; to know even one life has breathed easier because you have lived. **This is to have succeeded**.

Ralph Waldo Emerson (1803 – 82)

To live in a harmonious balance of commitments and pleasures is what I strive for.

Jane Rule

Promise to yourself to be so strong that nothing can disturb your peace of mind. To be too wise for worry, too tolerant for anger, and too courageous for fear. To Be Happy.

Author Unknown

Surprise and confound the world with your enthusiasm and optimism; **you know something they don't**.

G.W.F.

Your life is up to you. Life provides the canvas; you do the painting.

Author Unknown

Have a great life!

There is a theory which states that if ever anybody discovers exactly what the universe is for and why it is here, it will instantly disappear and be replaced by something even more bizarre and inexplicable.

There is another theory which states that this has already happened.

Douglas Adams,
The Hitchhiker's Guide to the Galaxy

APPENDIX

SUGGESTED READING

Gracious Living in A New World, ... Stoddard, Alexandra

Words of Wellness, ... Sutton, Joseph

The Heretics Handbook of Quotations, ... Bufe, Charles

Sunbeams, A Book of Quotations, ... Safransky, Sy

The Quotable Spirit, ... Mascetti, Manuela Dunn,
and Lorie, Peter

Chop Wood, Carry Water, ... Fields, Rick; Taylor, Peggy;
Weyler, Rex and Ingrasci, Rick

Worldwide Laws of Life, ... Templeton, John

Crazy Wisdom, ... Nisker, Wes "Scoop"

Self-Fulfillment, ... Kasparek, Don

A Dancing Star, ... Campbell, Eileen

Psycho-Cybernetics, ... Maltz, Dr. Maxwell

The Magic Power Of Self-Image Psychology, ...
Maltz, Dr. Maxwell

The Conquest Of Happiness, ... Russell, Bertrand

Psycho-Feedback, ... Thomas, Paul G.

My Favorite Quotes, ... Peale, Norman Vincent

You Can't Afford The Luxury Of A Negative Thought, ...
McWilliams, John-Roger and Peter

Life 101, ... McWilliams, John-Roger and Peter

The Treasury Of The Art Of Living ..... Greenberg, Sidney

Zen to Go .... Winokur, Jon

14,000 Things to Be Happy About .... Kipfer, Barbara Ann

Quotations of Wit and Wisdom ....
Gardner, John W. and Reese, Francesca Gardner

All Things Are Possible — Pass The Word ....
Orbach, Barbara Milo

Butterfly Kisses .... Bob Carlisle

Cats In The Cradle .... Harry Chapin

The Bug .... Mary-Chapin Carpenter

That's Life .... Frank Sinatra

I Take My Chances .... Mary-Chapin Carpenter

I Feel Lucky .... Mary-Chapin Carpenter

Daydream .... The Lovin' Spoonful

Mr. Businessman .... Ray Stevens

New York Minute .... Don Henley

The Heart Of The Matter .... Don Henley

Circle Of Life .... Elton John

One More Town .... The Kingston Trio

Centerfield .... John Fogarty

Both Sides Of The Story .... Phil Collins

He Went To Paris .... Jimmy Buffet

You Can't Always Get What You Want .... Rolling Stones

Blowin' In The Wind .... Bob Dylan

Superman .... Crash Test Dummies

Tin Man .... America

We May Never Pass This Way Again ...... Seals and Crofts

What A Wonderful World .... Louis Armstrong

New World In The Morning .... Roger Whittaker

Sunrise, Sunset .... Roger Whittaker

Miracles .... Don Williams, Jr.

Games People Play .... Joe South

I Never Promised You A Rose Garden .... Joe South

Walk A Mile In My Shoes .... Joe South

Raindrops Keep Falling On My Head .... B. J. Thomas

The Man In The Mirror .... Michael Jackson

Cabaret .... Liza Minnelli

Groovin' .... The Rascals

A Beautiful Morning .... The Rascals

In The Living Years .... Mike and The Mechanics

Run For The Roses .... Dan Fogleberg

St. Elmo's Fire .... John Parr

Another Day In Paradise .... Phil Collins

Fame .... Irene Cara

Thank God For Kids .... Oak Ridge Boys

Watching Scotty Grow .... Mac Davis

Life Is A Highway .... Tom Cochrane

Yellow Taxi .... Amy Grant

I've Got The Music In Me .... Kiki Dee

Imagine .... John Lennon

Time For Livin' .... The Association

One Tin Soldier .... Coven

I Got A Name .... Jim Croce

Teach Your Children Well .... Crosby, Stills and Nash

INDEX

C

H

R

215

T

218

*If after reading Timeless Wisdom you are not
fully satisfied, please detach the front cover and
mail it to*

*Cake Eaters, Inc.
14700 Village Square Place
Midlothian, VA. 23112*

with your address for a double refund.

REFLECTIONS

REFLECTIONS

REFLECTIONS

Timeless ✳ ☾ ✳
WISDOM

O R D E R   F O R M

CAKE EATERS INC. 14700 VILLAGE SQUARE PLACE, MIDLOTHIAN, VA 23112

——— 1-888-9WISDOM • FAX 804-355-4459 ———

QTY	PRICE	DESCRIPTION	TOTAL
	$ 9.95	*Timeless Wisdom Paperback*	
	$ 12.95	*Timeless Wisdom Hard Cover*	
	$ 29.95	*Timeless Wisdom, Limited Edition Leather Cover*	

Subtotal	
Sales Tax*	
Postage (If outside U.S.)	
TOTAL	

*VA residents add 4¹/₂%

Payment enclosed: ❑ Check ❑ Money Order   Please charge my: ❑ Mastercard ❑ Visa

Credit Card No._____ Exp. Date_____

Signature on Card_____

Your Name_____

Address_____

City_____State_____Zip_____

Phone *in case we need to call you regarding your order* Home_____Work_____

Canadian and foreign orders payable in U.S. Funds. Canadian and Mexican orders add $2.00 postage. Other foreign orders enclose $7.50 postage. Your order will be shipped surface rate unless special air fee arrangements are made. Make checks payable to Cake Eaters, Inc. Allow 2-3 weeks for delivery. Incomplete orders will be returned.

THE CRACK IN THE TEACUP

ALSO BY JOAN BODGER

How the Heather Looks

FOR CHILDREN

Belinda's Ball
Clever-Lazy
The Forest Family